MASTER BUILDER
JUNIOR

This book is available in quantity at special discounts for your group or organization.
For further information, contact:

Triumph Books LLC
814 North Franklin Street
Chicago, Illinois 60610
Phone: (312) 337-0747
www.triumphbooks.com

Printed in U.S.A.
ISBN: 978-1-62937-231-0

Content packaged by Mojo Media, Inc.
Joe Funk: Editor
Jason Hinman: Creative Director
Trevor Talley: Writer

Contents

▲ Sailor's Hideout by Shady og Ola.

Intro

Well, hello young Crafter!

What's that? You're not a Crafter yet? Or maybe you've played a little, mined a few mines, crafted a few...crafts, but you just want to get better at the game?

Oh, I see! Well, you're in luck then, because you just picked up the best guide in the world to becoming an amazing young Minecraft player!

▲ **Soon you'll have your own towers looking out over the wide Minecraft world.**

Minecraft is an awesome, thrilling, incredible, amazing (okay you get the point) video game that lets you have a grand adventure in a beautiful world that you get to shape yourself using the power of your imagination, not to mention a Pickaxe or two.

Minecraft is also the world's most popular video game, with over 100 million players around the globe, so it's no wonder you're interested in playing it yourself. Seems like just about everyone is grabbing a Pickaxe and Sword and heading out into this virtual world these days!

▲ **Sphere Tower of Doom by Chiknbiskit**

With this book, though, you're going to be way ahead of the game compared to everyone else you know. That's because this book is full of tips, tricks, advice, and even a secret or two about this game of blocks and building.

You'll find information on how to get started in the game, what to do when you're nice and settled in, how to find all of those rare and awesome items and materials you need, and even a chapter on minigames and playing Minecraft in new and exciting ways online! Plus, there's a full Gallery of Incredible Builds, absolutely crammed with some of the best and coolest stuff Crafters just like you from all over earth have built in this little game. It's pretty spectacular, but don't take our word for it—flip on over and take a look!

▲ **Kelestria by MrPorteEnBois**

In fact, why don't you turn the page, get settled in front of your computer, console, or tablet with Minecraft loaded up, and let's get mining! There's an entire universe out there of adventure and creation to explore and experience, and it's only limited by your own imagination.

It's time to Craft!

Your First Day in MINECRAFT

So, Here You Are!

It's your first day in Minecraft, and there's a wide world around you to explore and play in. But what do you do first?

There's just so much to do in Minecraft, it can be a little confusing at first. The Minecraft world can also be pretty dangerous, especially at night, and getting a good start on your first day is very important. The overall goal of your first day is to have enough resources and a good shelter to keep you safe before it gets dark, and these things take a little bit of work.

Don't worry though! We'll walk you through what to do so you have a great first day in your new favorite game.

The Three Keys to Your First Day

The first few moments in your Minecraft game should focus on the three most important things in Minecraft: resources, tools, and shelter.

Resources

Almost everything in Minecraft is made of blocks that can be "broken" and picked up, and you can use each thing to build with or to make other things. Gathering resources is very important to Minecraft, and you will need to get some very early on in your first day.

Tools

Tools are items that make tasks easier in Minecraft. For instance, there are Shovels to dig Dirt faster, Pickaxes to make mining Stone much faster and to let you get important ores (more on those later!), and many more tools. You'll build these using the resources you gather, and you need a few as quickly as you can get them in your first day.

Shelter

There are lots of creatures in Minecraft that want nothing more than to attack you, and it can be a little bit scary sometimes! Luckily, all you need to be safe is a nice home with walls, Doors, and some Torches to keep the place well lit and cozy. Making your first home is the final goal of your first day.

Step 1: Gathering Wood to Make Your First Items

You start off in Minecraft without any tools or items—it's just you and your fists against the world! Let's get started gathering resources.

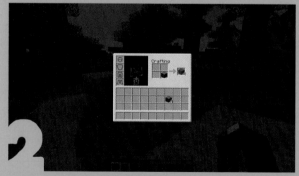

THE FIRST THING YOU WANT TO DO is to find a few trees so you can get some Wood to make your first tools and items.

POINT YOURSELF AT A BLOCK OF WOOD ON A TREE, and press and hold the attack button to "punch" the tree (this is usually the left mouse button on a computer or the right trigger on a console). When the block breaks, it will drop Wood, and you can walk over to pick it up.

GATHER AT LEAST 3 WOOD.

OPEN YOUR CRAFTING MENU, and put the 3 Wood into the empty spaces, and then turn them into Wood Planks.

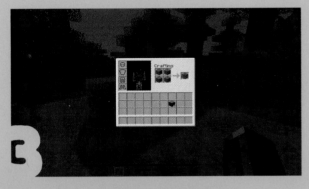

PUT ONE WOOD PLANK into each of the squares of the Crafting menu, and create a Crafting Table. This is one of the most important items in the game, as it's what lets you do the "crafting" part of Minecraft.

PLACE YOUR NEW CRAFTING TABLE on the ground, and use it to open a bigger Crafting menu. This is where we'll make your first tools and other items.

Step 2: Make Some Tools

What we need to do is to quickly gather more resources so we can build a house. To do that, we need a few handy tools.

1

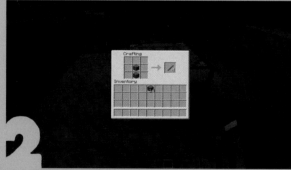

2

IN THE CRAFTING MENU for your Crafting Table, turn some Wood Planks into Sticks. Make sure you leave some Wood Planks though! If you need more Planks, go chop down a little more Wood. You can never have enough Wood on your first day!

NOW CREATE YOUR FIRST TOOL by using this pattern in your Crafting Table. This will make an Axe, which will help you chop down Wood much faster!

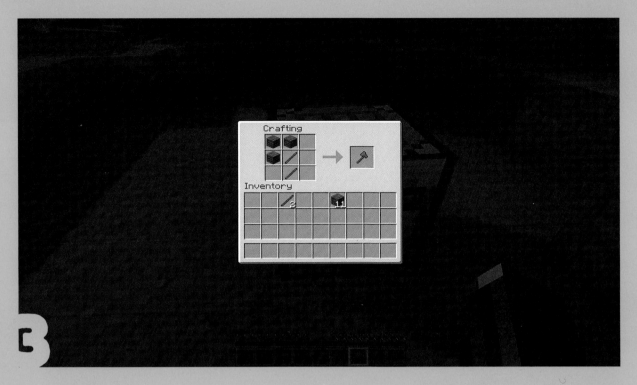

3

WE'RE ALSO GOING TO MAKE A WOODEN SWORD for protection and a Wooden Pickaxe to mine Cobblestone and ores.

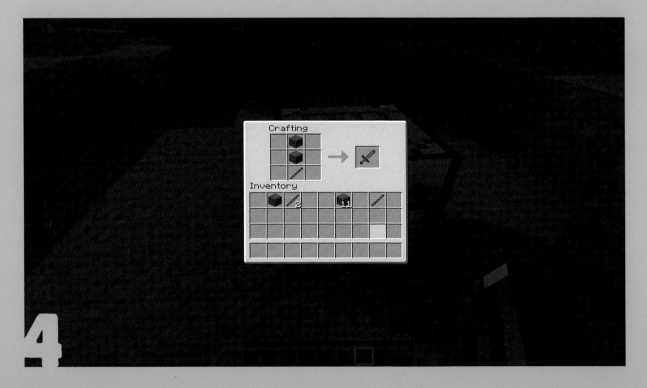

4

Step 3: Gather More Resources for Your Home

We need a few more things before we can start building a house to spend the night in.

FIRST, WE NEED SOME COBBLESTONE so we can make a Furnace. It's easy to find Stone to mine—either look for grey blocks out in the open, or just dig down with your hand or a Pickaxe. Don't dig straight down though; dig so that you're making a staircase downward.

WHEN YOU FIND STONE, mine about 10. Notice that it turns to Cobblestone when it breaks—this is a weaker version of Stone, but it's what we need right now.

ALSO BE ON THE LOOKOUT for any Stone blocks that have black specks in them. This is Coal, and it's what we'll use to make Torches later. If you see any of this, mine it too! Ignore every other color of speckled Stone for right now.

IF YOU SEE ANY ANIMALS in the area, like Cows, Chickens, Rabbits, Pigs, or (especially) Sheep, tap them with your Sword and get the resources they drop.

You need food to keep living in Minecraft, and in the beginning of the game, you'll get this from animals. Sheep also drop Wool, which is very important because it lets you make a Bed, which will let you skip over the dangerous nighttime.

MAKE SURE YOU HAVE AT LEAST 12 WOOD as well, so chop down a few more trees if you need to.

Step 4: Building a Home!

By this time in your game, it will be getting dark, or it will start to very soon. We need to build you a house before it gets actually dark, or you'll find yourself in a dangerous situation when the nighttime creatures come out!

Homes Need Three Things:

1. A light source

2. To be secure from the outside (no gaps in the walls or roof)

3. A Bed (eventually)

FIND A GOOD PLACE TO BUILD A HOME. This is going to be your first home, so don't go too far (you can always build another one later), but look for a nice spot near some trees to build. This will make it easier to gather resources later.

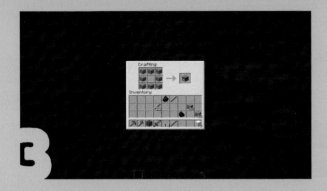

BUILD A SMALL RING OF WALLS around you with Wood Planks. Make this wall 2 blocks high, and make sure you have at least a space 6 blocks by 6 blocks in the middle. If you run out of Wood Planks, make a few more with your Crafting Table. Now you're a bit safer, but we need to do a few more things!

MASTER BUILDER
JUNIOR

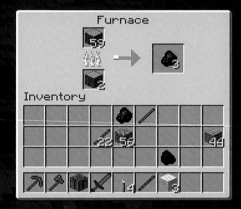

5

6

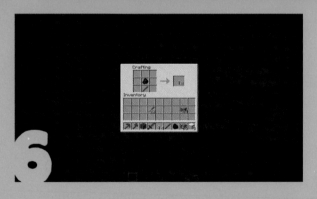

PLACE YOUR CRAFTING TABLE inside your walls, if you haven't already.

USE YOUR COBBLESTONE in your Crafting Table to build a Furnace, and then place this Furnace on the ground inside your walls too.

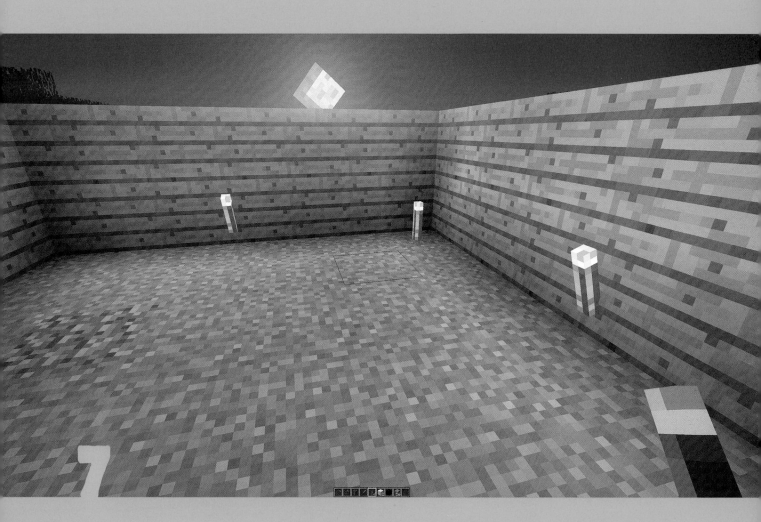

IN YOUR FURNACE, place a block of Wood into both empty slots. You'll see that the Furnace immediately starts burning: it is turning your Wood into Charcoal, which we can use like Coal to make Torches.

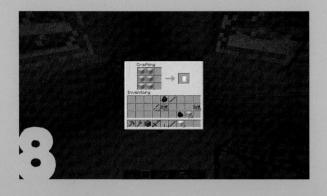

GO TO YOUR CRAFTING TABLE and place one Coal or Charcoal in the crafting grid above a stick. This makes a Torch! Make at least 5 Torches right now.

PLACE YOUR TORCHES on the ground or inside walls of your home.

GO BACK TO YOUR CRAFTING TABLE and build a Door with the recipe in image 8.

9

NOW, PUNCH OUT TWO BLOCKS in the wall of your home so there is a vertical gap two blocks tall, and place your Door into this gap.

FINALLY, FINISH YOUR HOME by making a roof of Wood Planks so that the only way into your home is through the Door.

10

GO BACK IN YOUR HOME, and you're now safe from the bad guys that will show up during the night, as well as from creatures like Creepers that can cause you trouble during the day!

The Next Step: Make Your Bed!

Ok, not "make your bed" the way your parents say to: we need to actually build you a Bed to sleep in!

 **HOT FACT:**

If you die at any time after you've slept in a Bed, you'll respawn right next to that Bed.

You should try to do it after you build your home if it's still light out. It can be kind of tricky, because you need to find three Sheep to collect 3 Wool for making your first Bed. Sheep aren't always around, so if you aren't able to find 3 Wool before it gets dark, head back home! You don't want to get stuck outside at night early in your game—that's a good way to take a Zombie punch to the face.

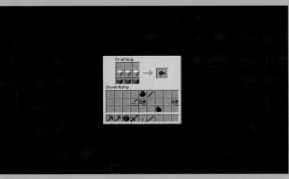

When you do get 3 Wool, use them and Wood Planks in your Crafting Table to make a Bed. You can then place the Bed in your home and use it to sleep right through the nighttime.

The World AROUND YOU

Hunting materials and items is a big part of your adventure in Minecraft. Whether you're a collector and just want all the different things in the game, or whether you've got a specific item you'd like to craft, chances are you're gonna want to find some unique block or item at some point.

That's where this part of the guide comes in. This is a quick breakdown of the different areas you can explore in the game, and what you might find there, plus some tips on finding the items everyone wants the most.

HOT FACT: There are actually many more biome variations than these! These are just the main ones, but you'll find all sorts of cool-looking landscapes in your Minecrafting journeys.

Biomes!

Look around you in the Minecraft world: have you noticed how each part of the Minecraft world has a distinct look, with specific plants and colors, and even different shapes of land? Each one of these different types of land in Minecraft is called a biome, and no matter where you are, you're in a biome!

Knowing about the different biomes is very helpful. It can help you know where to look for certain materials or items, and it can also help you find the coolest places to build!

Plains

The Plains (or Grasslands) is full of Grass, Flowers, and some smaller trees. It usually features plenty of mobs (both hostile and friendly) roaming about, and you can sometimes find caves, lakes, Villages, and Lava pools scattered around it.

What to get there: Grass, Tall Grass, Flowers/Sunflowers, Villages (which can contain many items), Horses

Master Builder Junior

Mesa

Dry and covered in beautiful bands of Clay and Sand of different types. These are pretty hard to find, but there's no better source of Clay in the game.

What to get there: Hardened Clay, six variations of Stained Clay, Red Sand/Sandstone, Cactus, Dead Bush

Forest

Trees, trees, and more trees! Another very common Biome, the Forest Biome is one of the most useful early in the game, as they provide large amounts of Wood.

What to get there: Flowers, all peaceful mobs, Mushrooms, Oak and Birch Trees

Desert

Sparse of life and resources, the Desert is pretty cool-looking, but is not a great place to spend large amounts of time unless it is near another, more resource-heavy Biome.

What to get there: Sand, Sandstone, Cactus, Dead Bushes, Sugar Cane, Desert Temples, and Villages (with many items each)

Swampland

Features short Oak Trees covered in Vines, and often has Mushrooms and Lily Pads around.

What to get there: Lily Pads, Vines, Clay, Mushrooms, Grass, Oak Trees, Witch Huts (and Witches!), Slimes

Extreme Hills

You'll know this one when you see it: huge hills with massive cliffs, overhangs, and even waterfalls.

What to get there: Flowers, Emeralds (the only biome they are in), Oak and Spruce Trees

Taiga

Can often be snowy and is a sort-of "Russian"-style forest with Spruce Trees and Wolves.

What to get there: Flowers, Ferns, Wolves, Spruce trees (in some variations there are also Podzol blocks and Mushrooms)

Jungle

BIIIIIG trees. Like, really, really big trees. And lots of them. Tons of foliage in general, and usually some hilly areas and lakes.

What to get there: Ferns, Flowers, Vines, Cocoa Pods, Melons, Jungle Temples (with various items and special blocks), Jungle Trees

Ocean

Lots and lots of Water, going off into the distance. There are also underwater Caves and Squids!

What to get there: Water, Squids (!)

Mushroom Island

Maybe the most unique Biome, this features purple-ish Mycelium as its primary building block and has Huge Mushrooms that look like trees. Always found out in the Ocean Biome.

What to get there: Mushrooms, Huge Mushrooms, Mycelium, Mooshrooms

Savanna

Somewhat like a Plains Biome with a few more short rises and falls, but with dry Grass and Acacia Trees. Like Plains, it can spawn Horses, and like a Desert, there's no rain on the Savanna.

What to get there: Tall Grass, Acacia Trees, Horses, other peaceful mobs, Villages (with many items)

Nether Dimension

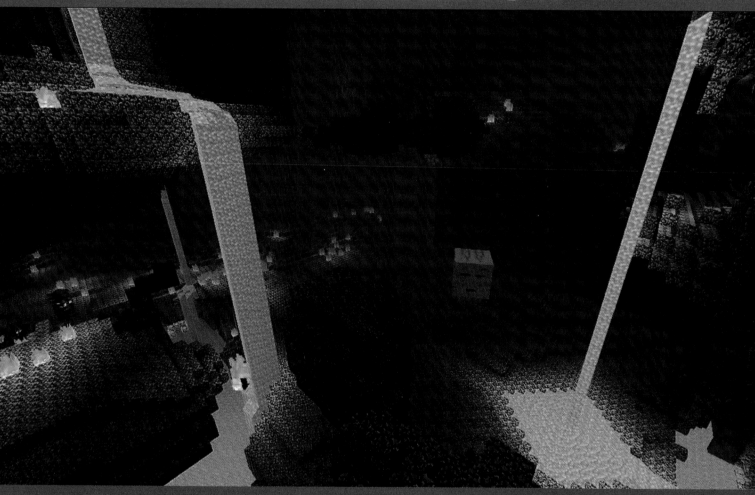

Fire, Lava, things trying to attack you constantly, little in the way of food. Basically super, super hostile.

What to get there: Netherrack, Nether Wart Glowstone, Soul Sand, Nether Brick, Nether Quartz, Magma Cubes, Ghasts, Blazes, Skeletons, Zombie Pigmen, Wither Skeletons, Nether Fortresses

End Dimension

The End is a spooky, but very cool dimension of islands floating in a sea of stars, and it's where Endermen live. It's also home to the dreaded Ender Dragon and the awesome End City, a special structure. This is actually the place where you can "beat" Minecraft by defeating the Ender Dragon. To get to The End, you'll need to use Ender Pearls (gotten from Endermen) in the End Portal found in Strongholds.

What to get there: End Stone, Chorus Plants, Purpur Block, Obsidian, Shulkers, Endermen, the Ender Dragon

STRUCTURES!

Sometimes in the different biomes in Minecraft, or deep underneath the ground, special buildings appear. These are called structures, and they are placed there in random locations by the world-creating program that makes your Minecraft world.

Structures are very important to know about, because each structure has its own look and contains treasures and unique items that make it very valuable to find. Whenever you find a structure in Minecraft, there's always something in it worth taking.

VILLAGES

If you're running around the Overworld (the part of the game that you spawn in), and you see a cluster of houses and think "Hey, I didn't build that!", you probably just found a Village. Villages are collections of buildings populated by neutral Villagers, and they usually have farms full of plants to steal, a Chest or two with good random items, and you can trade with the Villagers for other items.

STRONGHOLDS

At some point in the game, you'll either accidentally pop into one of these (often massive) structures, or you'll need to find one to get to The End. Strongholds can sometimes be small, but usually they're huge, confusing, and highly dangerous. There are only three Strongholds per world. Strongholds are super dangerous with many hostile mobs, but they also contain Chests of treasures (some of the rarest items in the game, like Golden Apples) and the portal to The End dimension. To find a Stronghold, you can throw Eyes of Ender and follow the path they fly off in (that's the direction of the Stronghold from where you are).

ABANDONED MINESHAFT

Randomly placed underground, especially intersecting with ravines and caves. Mineshafts are simply hallways, stairways, crossings, and rooms, often with Rail Tracks, supports and Minecarts in them. Probably the most dangerous place in the regular dimension, Mineshafts have many Spiders and poisonous Cave Spiders, but they also have a very large amount of Chests with treasure and lots of great items to grab. Plus, there's generally a whole lot of ore around!

DUNGEON

Small rooms randomly placed about the map, Dungeons contain a Monster Spawner and a Chest or two of super rare items. They're easier to clear out than the other underground structures, but Dungeons can still be very dangerous.

TEMPLES

Temples are awesome structures that look like big pyramids and contain Chests of useful items. Be careful though! Temples are trapped, so make sure you dig around to find the TNT blocks before they blow you up.

NETHER FORTRESSES

The only Structure found in the Nether, these are enormous, hugely dangerous, and are the only place to find Nether Wart and Blazes. They're not too hard to find, but getting out alive requires great gear, patience, and skill.

OCEAN MONUMENTS

A very difficult to find and harder to conquer underwater temple. They're protected by dangerous Guardians and have many rooms, the top one of which is filled with Gold Blocks. A pretty nice reward!

The Best
MATERIAL

Diamonds, Redstone, Emerald, oh my! Let's be honest: gathering resources is fun, but the most fun is finding awesome stuff like Diamonds and other rare items. There's nothing quite like finding those pockets of fancy, shiny ore in Minecraft, but it's just so hard sometimes. How about some tips, to help you out in your search?

MAKE SURE YOU'RE SEARCHING at the right level. To do this, check out our chart of the common levels to find ores in the Learning the Basics chapter, and then count up from the bottom of the world (the unbreakable Bedrock) to make sure you're in the right area.

DIG STAIRCASE TUNNELS TO THE BEDROCK. Staircase tunnels are an essential part of mining, because they give you a straight shot all the way down to the bottom level, which lets you count up to the right level. They also will generally run into caves and other structures that you can explore.

EXPLORE CAVES, RAVINES, MOUNTAINSIDES, and other natural structures where there's exposed Stone. Anywhere there's a bunch of exposed Stone, you're gonna find lots of ores, and you don't even have to dig!

LOOK (AND LISTEN) FOR LAVA.
Ores love to spawn around Lava pockets, but be careful you don't fall in!

WHEN YOU'RE AT THE RIGHT LEVEL FOR AN ORE, just dig straight out in a line. Eventually, you should find some good stuff if you stay on the right level.

Dying for some awesome Horse Armor, or a tasty Golden Apple? The rarest items in the game are all found in Chests in the different structures of Minecraft. Looking for and exploring structures is one of the biggest adventures in the game, but it can sometimes take a while to find!

FRIENDS & FOES
THE CREATURES OF MINECRAFT

▲ IRON GOLEM

It only takes a few seconds in Survival Mode to realize that your character in Minecraft is not alone. Nope, the world of Minecraft is a full one, filled with everything from tiny Chickens to Wolves to Zombie Pigmen to the giant Ghast, and if you're going to thrive in this crowded land, you're gonna need to know a bit about these creatures, known as "mobs."

Peaceful Mobs

▲ MOOSHROOM

▲ VILLAGER

There are quite a few mobs out there that won't ever attack you, no matter how many times pester them. These mobs are considered "peaceful." Peaceful mobs are super important because most of them drop special items, and they're often hunted for this reason (especially for their food drops).

 CHICKEN

🔥 HOT FACT:

Sheep don't have to be attacked with a sword to get Wool from them: you can use Shears on a Sheep and it will get the Wool and leave the Sheep alive. You can also dye Sheep with different dyes to get different colors of Wool.

Here's a list of the all the peaceful mobs and what you can get from them:

- **BAT:** No drops! Just cute.
- **CHICKEN:** Feathers, Raw Chicken
- **COW:** Leather, Raw Beef
- **DONKEY/MULE/HORSE:** Leather
- **MOOSHROOM:** Leather, Raw Beef, Mushroom Stew (If you use a bowl on them. Very awesome as a food source!)

 PIG

🔥 HOT FACT:

Iron and Snow Golems can be created! To build an Iron Golem, stack four Iron Blocks in a "T" shape and put a pumpkin on the top middle block. For Snow Golems, stack two Snow Blocks on top of each other, and plop a Pumpkin on the top. Now you've got two new friends!

- **OCELOT:** No drops, but you can tame them and turn them into a Cat! Adorable, but also helpful: Creepers are very scared of Cats and will stay away from them.
- **PIG:** Raw Porkchop
- **RABBIT:** Raw Rabbit, Rabbit Hide, Rabbit's Foot
- **SHEEP:** Wool, Raw Mutton
- **SQUID:** Ink Sac
- **WOLF:** None, but can be tamed and made a pet Dog! Dogs can follow you, and they can be set to attack creatures that attack you or that are around the area.

▲ SNOW GOLEM

▲ ZOMBIE PIGMAN

- **IRON GOLEM:** Iron Ingot, Poppy. These big guys are great guardians and will fight hostile mobs, which you'll often see them doing in Villages.
- **SNOW GOLEM:** Snowballs, Pumpkin. Another guardian mob, they'll pelt anything that attacks you with furious Snowball flurries.
- **VILLAGER:** None, but you can trade with them for special items!
- **ZOMBIE PIGMAN:** Rotten Flesh, Gold Nugget, will rarely drop Gold Ingots

Hostile Mobs

▲ CREEPER

▲ SKELETON

Now, these are the guys in Minecraft who want nothing more than to bite you, poison you, shoot you full of arrows, and otherwise attempt to make you no more.

Even with the best gear, a few of these guys ganging up on you can mean a quick defeat, especially if you don't know their tendencies and weaknesses. Get familiar with these guys as much as possible, and it most definitely will save your life.

▲ CAVE SPIDER

Hostile Mobs:

- **BLAZE:** Blaze Rods, Glowstone Dust
- **CAVE SPIDER:** String, Spider Eye
- **CREEPER:** Gunpowder, Music Disc (if you can get a Skeleton to kill it), Creeper Head (if a Charged Creeper that has been hit by lightning kills another Creeper)
- **ELDER GUARDIAN/GUARDIAN:** Prismarine Shard, Prismarine Crystals, Raw Fish, Wet Sponge, Raw Salmon, Pufferfish, Clownfish

- **ENDER DRAGON:** TONS of experience, and the exit portal to The End
- **ENDERMAN:** Ender Pearl
- **GHAST:** Ghast Tear, Gunpowder
- **MAGMA CUBE:** Magma Cream
- **SILVERFISH:** None! These guys are just annoying and dangerous.
- **SKELETON:** Arrow, Bone, Skeleton Skull (if killed by a Charged Creeper)
- **SLIME:** Slimeball

 **WITCH**

🔥 HOT FACT:

Each hostile mob has its own special attack and movement style. For instance, Skeletons shoot arrows and walk back and forth but keep their distance, while Zombies will walk directly toward you and will call other Zombies to them. Pay close attention to each mob that you fight, and learn to use their behaviors against them to defeat them every time.

- **SPIDER:** String, Spider Eye
- **WITCH:** Glass Bottle, Glowstone Dust, Gunpowder, Redstone, Spider Eye, Stick, Sugar
- **WITHER:** Nether Star
- **WITHER SKELETON:** Coal, Bone, Wither Skeleton Skull (if killed by Charged Creeper)
- **ZOMBIE:** Rotten Flesh, Zombie Head (if killed by Charged Creeper), will rarely drop Iron Ingots, Carrots, or Potatoes

 A pair of towers sits atop an Extreme Hills Biome.

Learning THE BASICS

After your first awesome day in Minecraft, it should be pretty clear: there's a LOT to do in this game! Now that you can ride out the dangerous night inside your cool new house, you've got the freedom to start playing the game however you like.

It's a big world out there and while there are no rules telling you what you have to do, this chapter's all about the most popular and exciting things you can do in Minecraft. It'll teach you the basics of everything from mining to crafting (and more!), so let's get started.

🔥 HOT FACT:

Each Minecraft world is different, but every one is as big as the entire surface of the earth. You can try to walk to the edge of it, but it would take you as long as it would take to walk around our whole planet!

Explore

You can't do much in Minecraft without exploring a bit! There's just so much to see in Minecraft: from tall, tall mountains to creepy caves, to a Lava waterfall or two.

Explore Like a Pro

Before you set out into the big, wide world of your Minecraft universe, it's a good idea to do some preparation. You could always just start walking of course, but trust us: this will lead to you getting very lost very soon. To be a pro explorer, you should do three things:

SET A GOAL! Are you looking for something in particular in your Minecraft world, like a place for a new base or a certain material to mine, or are you exploring just for fun? Whatever your goal, it's a good idea to think about it just a bit before you go, so you can prepare the right way.

GEAR UP FOR YOUR TRIP! There's nothing more important before you take a walkabout in your Minecraft world than taking the right items with you. You want to make your chances of surviving your trip and achieving your goal the best they can be, and that's all about items.

Here's the best items to take:

3-10 food items

At least 30 Cobblestone and Wood (for shelters and item crafting)

30-64 Dirt (if you fall in a hole or get lost, stack them on top of each other while jumping to get up higher)

At least 15 Torches

2-3 Pickaxes (Stone or better)

2 Swords (Stone or better)

The best armor you can make

A Bed (it's best to sleep through the night when exploring, if you can)

▲ **A simple spawn point beacon**

BE SMART! Smart exploration basically involves two things: making sure you're safe and keeping track of where you are.

To stay safe, try not to explore at night, and when night does fall, build yourself a small shelter and use your Bed to sleep through it until it's light again.

Keeping from getting lost is a bit harder, but there are a couple of options. One, you can craft a Map to show you where you are. And two, you can mark a trail by setting Torches down as you go, or by building tall Dirt towers. When you need to go back, just follow them the other way.

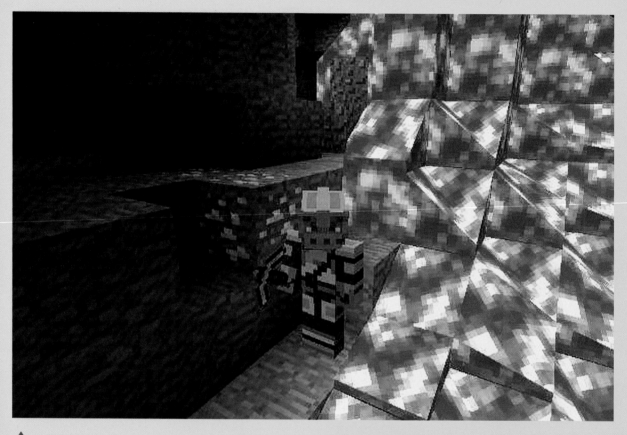

▲ A proud miner stands by his Diamonds.

Mine (and Gather)!

Mining and gathering resources are super important to Minecraft. Mining is dangerous and takes a lot of time, thinking, and resources to do, so it's important to learn a few tips and tricks to make it easier.

Look in the Right Place

Plan your mining and gathering trips around what resources you're looking for. Not everything is found near everything else, so when you look for resources, plan to go for certain groups you know will be near each other. For instance, when you go chopping Wood, it's a great time to hunt peaceful mobs and to collect surface items like Flowers or Wheat Seeds from Grass.

Ore-mining is one of the hardest things to do, because you usually have to dig a lot to find rare ores like Diamonds. Here's an easy chart, though, that will tell you the "level" each type of ore is most often found on (meaning how many blocks up from the bottom layer of your world they will spawn).

Ore type	Most Likely to Find On Layers	Highest Layer Common On
Coal	5-52	Layer 128
Iron	5-54	Layer 64
Lapis Lazuli	14-16	Layer 23
Gold	5-29	Layer 29
Diamond	5-12	Layer 12
Redstone	5-12	Layer 12
Emerald	5-29	Layer 29
Nether Quartz	15-120	Layer 120

Screenshot: Minecraft® ™ & © 2009–2016 Mojang/Notch.

▲ Another shot of a good mining camp, complete with Chests, a Crafting Table, and a furnace.

Take the Right Gear With You

Just like exploring, you gotta take the right stuff with you when you go to gather resources, or you're gonna run into trouble! Make sure you have everything from our basic exploring kit, plus take at least one Chest on any trip where you'll be mining or gathering a lot. Instead of keeping all of your resources that you're gathering in your inventory, put the Chest near where you're gathering and place the items in there. This way if something bad happens, your items will be safe and won't disappear (items disappear after five minutes on the ground).

🔥 HOT TIP:

Not every tool will mine every ore block! You need tools made of certain materials to get certain ores, so memorize this chart to know exactly what tool will break the block you want.

Ore type	Lowest quality tool needed to drop (will drop with any higher quality tool as well)
Coal	Wooden Pickaxe
Iron	Stone Pickaxe
Lapis Lazuli	Stone Pickaxe
Gold	Iron Pickaxe
Diamond	Iron Pickaxe
Redstone	Iron Pickaxe
Emerald	Iron Pickaxe
Nether Quartz	Wooden Pickaxe

Mine Smart

Here are some expert tips to make sure you get the most out of your mining experience:

Don't mine without weapons and armor. You never know when you'll be attacked, or fall!

Take frequent trips back to base, or make a mini-base near your gathering spot. The longer you wait to go back, the more likely you'll lose all of your stuff.

Pay attention to the area around you. Don't fall in holes, step in Lava, or run into a Creeper! Keep an eye out, and mine/gather with a buddy if you can.

Try new areas if you can't find what you want. Looking for caves is especially helpful when mining ore, as you can just run through them looking for exposed pieces of ore.

▲ You're just a few menus away from your first mine.

Craft!

Just about every item in the game can either be made with other items or is used to make other items itself, and some are both!

There are dozens and dozens of items you can make, and learning the various combinations and recipes is part of the fun of Minecraft. There are five main "stations" that you can have in the game to build different items, each of which does a different thing.

THE TRUSTY CRAFTING TABLE: The Crafting Table is the primary station where you'll be doing your crafting in the world of Minecraft. It creates all sorts of hugely important items, including but not limited to tools, weapons, armor, other crafting stations, decorations, doors, and Redstone items. You'll be using this one a lot!

THE BREWING STAND: This very special station is extremely difficult to build! You have to defeat a dreadful Blaze and get a Blaze Rod to create it, but once you do, the Brewing Stand will allow you to craft Potions. Potions give your character temporary powers, like breathing underwater or hitting harder, and they're very useful but can cost a lot of resources to make.

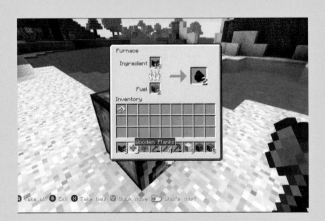

THE FURNACE: The Furnace makes raw ore into ore ingots you can use, cooks food, and creates Charcoal for Torches.

THE ENCHANTMENT TABLE: Another station you'll get later in your game when you have already explored a lot, the Enchantment Table adds powers to your tools, weapons, and armor. It can do things like make armor fireproof or make a Sword do more damage. It uses experience (the green bar and number by your item tray) to do this. **Be careful: if you die, all of your experience goes away, so this is yet another reason to always go prepared!**

THE ANVIL: The Anvil is an item that is used to repair other items like tools, weapons, and armor, which is super useful when it comes to expensive items like Diamond Swords and armor. You can also use it to combine enchantments, making even more powerful items than with the Enchantment Table alone.

▲ A random Creeper attack is a common thing when exploring in Minecraft.

Fight!

Unless you've got your world set to Peaceful Mode, you're not going to survive long in Minecraft without having to battle the hostile mobs of your world. While combat in Minecraft isn't as complicated as many other games, it's still pretty tricky, and these tips should help you survive long enough to run away or defeat your foes.

▲ **This Crafter has a much better chance of surviving because of her gear.**

SPEND RESOURCES ON GOOD GEAR. It might be tempting to save up those Diamonds you took so long to find and mine, but trust us: it's worth spending on good armor, weapons, and tools. The better your gear, the longer you'll stay alive and the faster you'll get more resources to get even more good gear.

◆ A young Crafter prepares to go out into battle with a Diamond Sword and enchanted armor.

PRACTICE WITH THE BOW AND THE SWORD. Weapons in Minecraft seem simple, but getting good at them really does take practice! When you know you're safe (such as when you don't have many items on you and only see one hostile mob), try a bit of combat when you can to learn how to use both weapons. The Bow especially can be useful.

▲ This Crafter is using his strong Obsidian Nether Portal to hide from the blasts of the terrifying Ghast.

USE THE LAND AND THE GAME TO YOUR ADVANTAGE. Since you can destroy and build in Minecraft, use this in combat to defeat your foes easier. For instance, mobs can't duck, so if you can dig out the block by a mob's feet while there are still blocks between you and its head, it won't be able to shoot or hit you if it's close, but you can hit it.

▲ Putting a wall between the Crafter and the Creeper will save you over and over.

DON'T GET INTO A FIGHT YOU CAN'T WIN. This is the most important lesson! If you don't have a lot of health or good gear, or you're outnumbered, run away! It's not worth losing your items and experience to try and fight, and you'll almost always lose in these circumstances.

Screenshot: Minecraft® ™ & © 2009–2016 Mojang/Notch.

▲ This absolutely enormous farm is set up to automatically harvest Wheat with Water.

Farm!

Resources are out there all over the wild in Minecraft, but sometimes you just wanna eat a Steak and not have to go find a Cow. At some point in your game, starting a farm is a great idea to make finding food a whole lot easier.

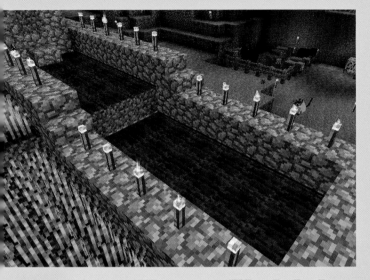

Hoe Those Fields! Farming Plants

There used to just be a few plants you could farm in Minecraft, but now all of the versions have quite a few. Though there are some differences between the various plants, all of them require the following to farm:

1. A Dirt block to plant on (Melons and Pumpkins require two, one next to the other) that has been hoed (use a Hoe on it).

2 Water within four blocks on the same level or one level above.

3. Light, either from the sun or from a block or item (Torch, Glowstone, etc.).

4. Time. Every plant grows at a different rate depending on conditions and computer randomization, but all of them take time. That is, unless you have some Bonemeal, which can be used on plants to make them grow very fast.

Wrangle Cows! Breeding Animals

The fuzzy friends that are peaceful mobs in Minecraft can often be tamed and bred to make more mobs! Whether you just want a bunch of friends, or you're looking for a way to have your own meat ranch outside your home, breeding animals is a useful trick. To breed mobs, you'll need to find them in the wild and feed them the correct item until you see hearts above their head, which means they are looking to breed. The item that makes these guys breed will also make them follow you, which is very useful for putting them in pens or trapping them in your home.

Here's what item lets you breed which mob:

Note: Ocelots and Wolves are made into pets when you feed them Bones (for the Wolf) or Raw Fish (Ocelot)! You'll need to do this before breeding them.

MOB	BREEDING ITEM	OTHER USABLE ITEMS
• Horse	• Golden Apple • Golden Carrot	Sugar, Wheat, Apples, Golden Carrots, Golden Apples, and Hay Bales will make them grow faster and heal
• Sheep • Cow • Mooshroom	Wheat	Wheat will make them grow faster
• Pig	• Carrots *Pocket Edition only* • Potatoes • Beetroots	Carrots will make Pigs grow faster
• Chicken	• Seeds *Pocket Edition only* • Pumpkin seeds • Melon seeds • Beetroot seeds	None
• Tamed Wolves (dogs)	Any type of meat, whether cooked, raw, or rotten	Make sure your Wolf/Dog is at full health before breeding, which you also do by feeding it
• Tamed Ocelots (cats)	• Raw Fish • Raw Salmon • Clownfish • Pufferfish	None
• Rabbits	• Dandelions • Carrots • Golden Carrots	None

Build!

Something's definitely changed about Frosty from his days as a cartoon to this towering, hungry-lookin' version.

As you might know already from some of the photos of the absolutely amazing things people have built in Minecraft, building is one of the most fun and imaginative things you can do in Minecraft.

Using all of the different blocks and items available, people out there have created pretty much everything you can think of—and not just buildings! We've seen every kind of building of course, from soaring castles to beautiful mansions, but we've also seen everything in Minecraft from dragons to space ships to pirate boats to replicas of real-life cities and beyond. Becoming a stellar builder takes practice, but here are some tips to get you on your path to being a master builder.

PLAN YOUR BUILDS FIRST by sketching them out with cheap blocks. It's hard to know if a build will fit in an area unless you go ahead and place the blocks, so use things like Dirt to sketch out your build before beginning.

▲ Another architecturally sound build, Avaricia is one that shows just what shaders can do to a room that's well-lit.

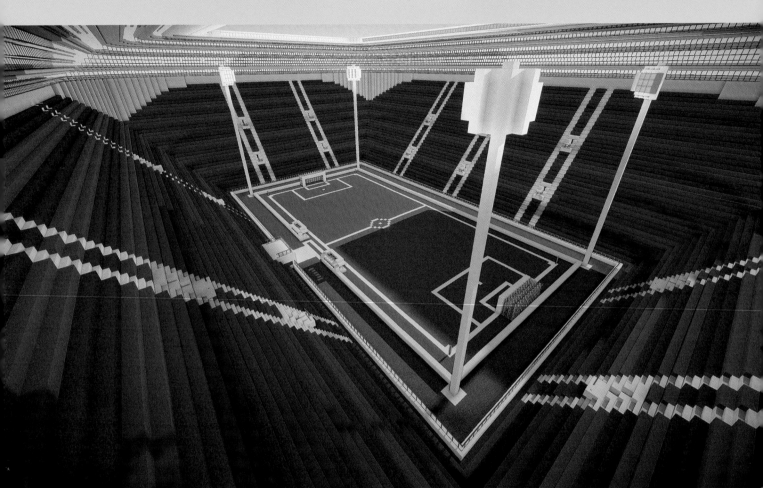

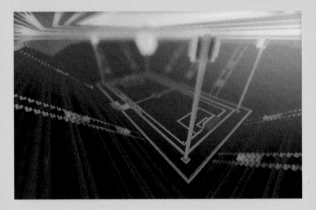

GET CREATIVE WITH ITEMS AND BLOCKS. Just because a block or item is "supposed" to be something like Stone or a Fence doesn't mean it has to be in your build. Use blocks and items that look like what you want to create (like, say, stacking Fences to make a flag pole and using Wool for the flag), and be creative!

▲ The details like the massive light poles, the detailing on the semi-enclosed roof, the curved corners of the structure, and the entrance and exit tunnels make this one of the best stadiums we've ever seen in Minecraft.

TRY COPYING THINGS YOU SEE ONLINE or in this book to get better.
Nothing will make you a great builder faster than copying something cool you've seen, because you'll have to think hard to make it look right.

Playing Minecraft
ONLINE MINIGAMES, SERVERS, AND MORE FUN

Since the earliest days of Minecraft, creative folks out there have been taking the rules of this blocky building game and have made entirely new games out of it! These are called minigames, and there are many, many different kinds of them. Some of these minigames are amazing, and you can play all of them online on servers for free.

Check out some of these awesome minigames, and then take a look at our list of some of the best servers around where you can go play these and tons of other super fun games right now.

Paintball

Flying Snowballs are a common sight in Paintball; in fact you'll probably never see so many in the air at once anywhere else in Minecraft!

Paintball is pretty easy to pick up: all you do is run around a map trying to hit players with "paintballs," which are actually just Snowballs under a different name. If you hit a player once, they are immediately warped back to spawn and you and your team get points. The first team to get a certain amount of points or the team with the most points after a set amount of time wins. On some servers getting "kills" earns you coins that you can use to purchase power ups for either you or your team, like a triple-shot or reducing the amount of deaths your team has.

Survival Games

▲ **Players in a server match of Survival Games wait for the clock to countdown so they can rush to the weapon chests in the center of the map.**

Perhaps the most popular game people have created within Minecraft, Survival Games involves special maps that have been created for combat. Based on the *Hunger Games*, the idea is that a group of players start the game near a bunch of chests filled with various items. At a signal, all players rush the items and try to grab as many as they can without getting defeated, while also attacking other players.

TNT Run

▲ A game of TNT Run gets very exciting and complicated when just a few players (and blocks to stand on) are left.

TNT
Run has been around for a long time, and it involves running around in an arena on a flat surface which will fall out underneath you as you go. That means that if you step on a block, you better move quick because soon that block will drop and you'll fall to the next layer below. The idea is to keep moving around and create holes in the ground as you move that other players fall into. Since these players are creating more holes themselves, you'll need to keep on your toes and plan out where you run, jumping any holes that you can't run around.

Hide N Seek

▲ A group of hiders rush to find good spots before the seeker is released.

Similar to the real-world game, but in Minecraft Hide N Seek, the hiders have an extra advantage in that they appear to the seekers to look like regular blocks in the game! So, for instance, a hider might look like an Oak Wood block or a Fence post or a Glowstone lamp. These maps are usually made so that there are a lot more of the type of block you choose to be, and seekers have a certain amount of time to find all of the hiding blocks. If the hiders make it through the time limit without being found and defeated, they win!

Parkour

▲ **This parkour map is Assassin's Creed themed. There are many, many different types of parkour maps out there, and each has its own challenges and theme.**

Parkour is probably the easiest minigame to learn the rules of, but one of the very hardest to master. All you're trying to do in Parkour is to jump from block to block on a pre-made course while not falling. If you fall, the courses are set up so that you have to start over at the beginning, and if you make it to the end, you win!

Spleef

▲ **Spleef is one of the oldest minigames in Minecraft, and it's still one of the most popular!**

Spleef is wild, and it's pretty simple: a one-block-thick layer of Wool sits above a pool of Lava in an arena constructed of tough materials (such as Obsidian). Players start on top of the layer of Wool in the corners of the arena and use Flint and Tinder, Fire Charges, or even a Bow to light the Wool on fire or shoot it out. When the Wool breaks, it disappears, leaving gaps in the floor through which players can fall. The last player who has stayed out of the Lava wins!

The Walls

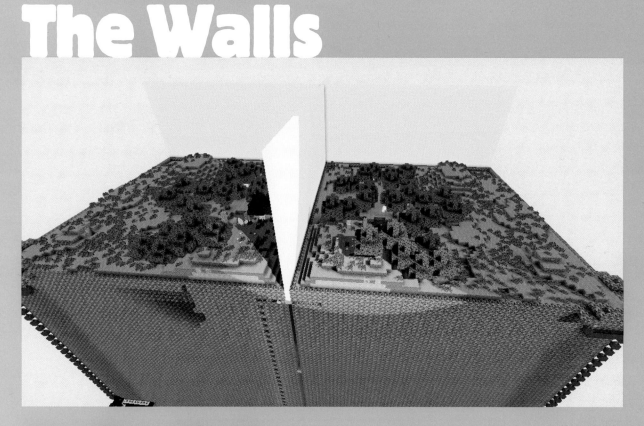

▲ **A group of players on a server prepare to enter The Walls.**

You and 3 other players or teams are dropped into one section of a Minecraft world that has limits (meaning it's only so big). There are giant sand walls dividing your quadrant of the map from the other players, and a huge timer floating above everything. You have until the timer reaches 0:00 to prepare yourself and your area for battle, and once the timer does hit zero, the walls fall down! At that point, it's an all-out brawl to see who can live the longest, and whoever does wins!

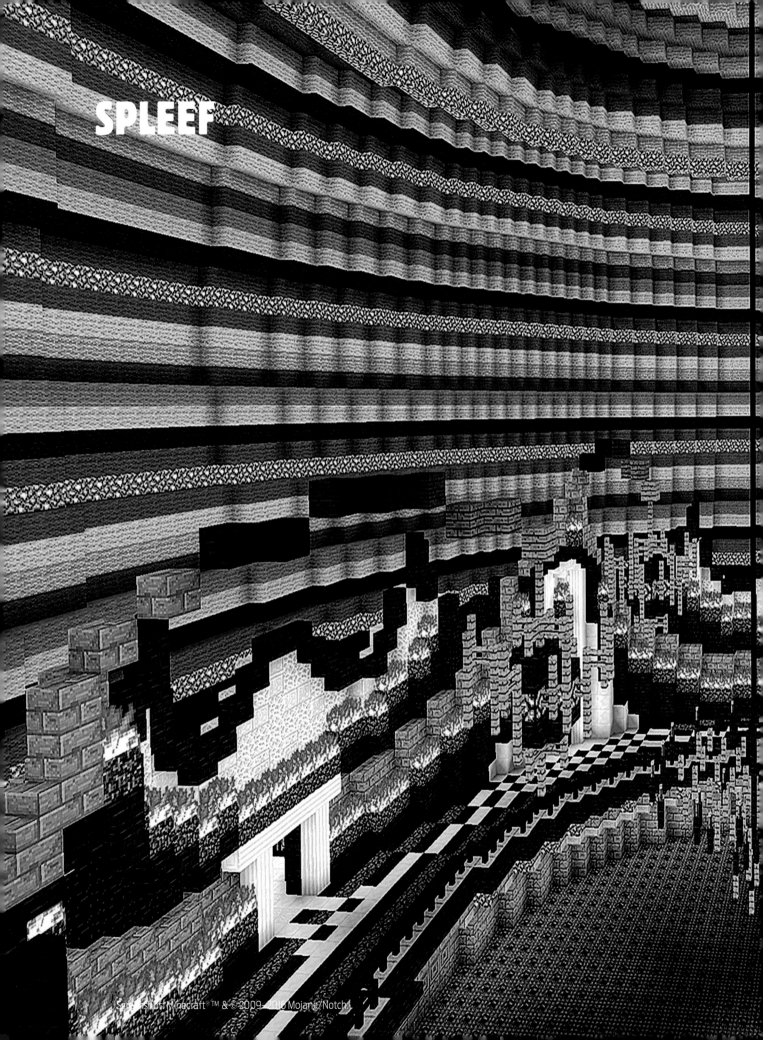

SPLEEF

SOME AWESOME SERVERS TO CHECK OUT!

There are literally thousands and thousands of Minecraft servers out there, and some of them are really popular with over 10,000 people on them at one time. You'll probably find one you like the best, but to get you started, here's a short list of some of the most popular ones, and the address where you can find them.

Note: Be careful when going on public servers! Make sure you ask your parents first before you sign on, because there are a lot of other real people on these. Most of them are very nice, but practice good judgment and stay safe.

Arkham Network

Server Address:
mc.arkhamnetwork.org

The Arkham Network consistently comes up in best-of lists for Minecraft servers because it is one of the most well-oiled and fun competitive servers that exist today.

▲ One of the best parts of big servers like Arkham network is that everything from the hub to the minigame maps is professionally designed and looks amazing.

Hypixel

Server Address: mc.hypixel.net

The great Hypixel's personally hosted server, hypixel. net is another quality competition/PvP server and one of the more frequented servers period online.

▲ Few servers can boast either hubs as gorgeous, or minigames as fun and creative, as Hypixel's.

Mineplex

Server Address: us.mineplex.com

A top minigame server, Mineplex typically is one of the very busiest servers, often with over 10,000 players online at a time.

Here you see the team select for the awesome Mineplex Arcade, and the image above is of one of the featured games. In this game every player looks like a Villager in a sea of real Villagers. You have to try and figure out who is real and every so often everyone changes into their normal form for a few seconds. Super fun!

Treasure Island

▲ **Treasure Island takes Creative Mode quite seriously, as is readily apparent when you spend a little time around the 0,0 coordinates, where most of the oldest and best plots are located.**

Server Address: ticreative.org

Treasure Island is actually a collection of servers, like many of the others on this list, and it hosts many of the popular styles from PvP to Skyblock, but we're focusing on the subserver that focuses on Creative Mode. This is because the Treasure Island Creative server is incredible when it comes to the amount and quality of builds that can be found there.

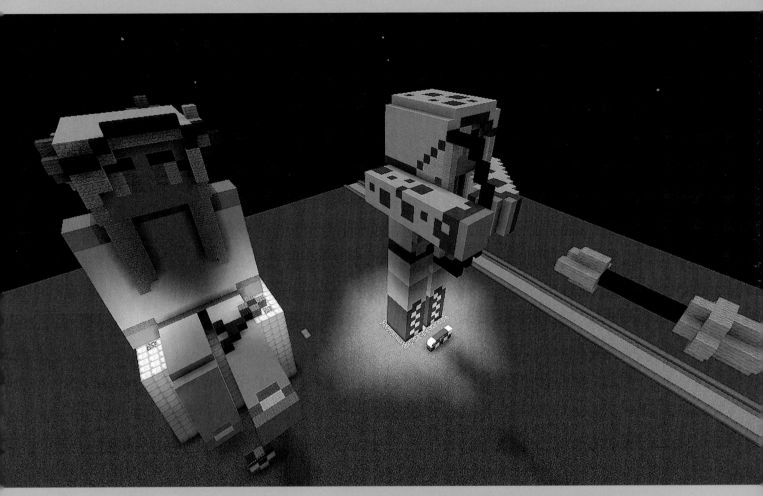

Lichcraft

▲ Lichcraft is a server that has just about every major mode and does all of it well.

Server Address: us.lichcraft.com

Consistently ranked among the top servers online, Lichcraft is similar to Hypixel and the Arkham Network but with a few different games to play, including Survival, Skygrid, KitPvP, Duels, Prison, MineZ, and excellent Factions servers that are well-populated and nicely run.

LICHCRAFT

The Gallery Of INCREDIBLE BUILDS

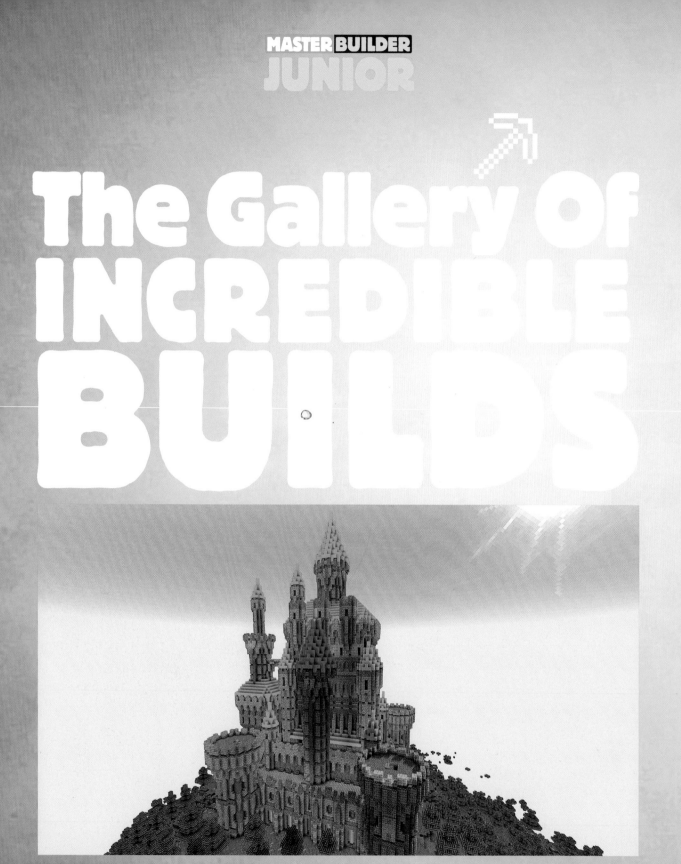

CASTLE HILL • BY: AANDOLAF: Aandolaf says that the inspiration for this castle came partly from the castle that inspired that of Sleeping Beauty, known as the Neuschwanstein Castle.

CLOUDHAVEN • BY: LYNCHYING: CloudHaven is almost definitely the most jam-packed ship we've ever seen that still looks like it was professionally designed. There is a cool set of challenges associated with this map, mostly based around trying to survive and finding things in the ship like the treasury room, which is a cool twist on the standard steampunk sky map.

DESERT CITY OF ALKAZARA! • BY: JERACRAFT:
A stupendous green-domed palace towers over this city, but there's so much more to see. Wander the streets and you'll find a city that almost seems to live and breathe, including everything from homes to farms to docks to towers.

ELBANE'S ARRIVAL • BY: MRD4NNY: The very first time we loaded up Elbane's Arrival, we didn't really know how big Elbane the dragon would be, or where it would be. When we turned around and had this huge thing loading up right behind us, all fangs and glowing eyes, it actually put fear into us!

FORBIDDEN CITY • BY: BOHTAURI: This stunning build is a replica of the Forbidden City in China, and builder bohtauri replicated it almost 100% to scale!

ROMECRAFT COLOSSEUM • BY: STUGACE: A perfect ellipse built with cubes? Yep, that's the Romecraft Colosseum, a build that was meant to be as close to a real life colosseum as possible, and which draws heavy influence from the Colosseum in Rome.

THIEVES' FORT • BY: MACKMO: Also known as Forest Manor, the Thieves' Fort is a lesson in the idea that fantasy doesn't necessarily have to look completely out of this world, but can instead resemble something very realistic.

GREENFIELD • BY: THEJESTR, KRISTOFFERANDRE, TRIPPLEX, AND TEAM: This is one of the most famous builds in Minecraft, with over 1 million total views on Planet Minecraft, and it is just huge. It has been under construction for years, and it includes just about every kind of neighborhood, district, and feature of a city you can think of.

OASIS OF THE SEAS TERMINAL 18
BY: CHARLESGOLDBURN: CharlesGoldburn is almost unquestionably Minecraft's premier cruise boat builder. Among his many, many boats he has painstakingly recreated in Minecraft in a 1:1 scale (meaning they are as big in Minecraft as they are in real life) is the Oasis of the Seas boat, in this build seen at a docking terminal.

SOVIET SSGN-941 TYPHOON NUCLEAR SUBMARINE
BY: KANOVALOV: In Russian, the name for this map is "Tsel' unichtozhena!" which means, "Target eliminated!" With firepower like this beast commands, it's a phrase that you can easily imagine echoing off its metal walls when you walk through the SSGN-941.

ARENDELLE CASTLE • BY: ILIKECUTEPEOPLE: Anyone who has seen the ridiculously popular movie *Frozen* should recognize this build: the Arendelle Castle. This thing goes above and beyond by including not just the castle itself, but all of the surrounding land, and there are even some pretty cool little extra bits in this one like ships and some builds up in the (very nicely built) hills. Going even more above and beyond, there are actually two versions of this build, one in the summer and one, appropriately, in the winter.

USS EXCELSIOR, USS ENTERPRISE & USS RELIANT
BY: MOZZIE: This Star Trek build is straight-up killer. It faithfully recreates the ships from the films and show and their construction bays, and is actually walkable inside, which most Trek builds aren't.

PARKOUR MAP CHRISTMAS CALENDAR
BY: MINECRAFT-PG5: The "Christmas Calendar" part of this map refers to the fact that there's a different parkour run that you can open up one by one, like those Christmas calendars with the chocolates in them, but you can enjoy this map whenever you wish!

WORKING FOOSBALL TABLE • BY: SETHBLING: This build is quite big and looks very much like a real table, and it uses Water that is activated around a player's "men" when the button corresponding with that man is pressed to shove a "ball" around (an item that is pushed by the Water).

PROGRAMMABLE DRUM KIT • BY: DISCOOOOOOO: This addition to Disco's Minecraft band setup has three different channels with 16 steps each, and different drums on it can be muted and defined as you like. It's even animated!

CASTELLUM ROMANORUM • BY EDSINGER: Server hubs come in all shapes, sizes, and even time periods, this one being an ancient Roman/fantasy castle-inspired build. It's a very big hub, and one that could house a lot of portals to different parts of a server, and it has a very mature look to it that many hubs don't.

ARENDELLE CASTLE

DIRT HOUSE • BY CARLOTTA4TH: Apparently on some Minecraft servers, saying "I built a dirt house today" is a common thing to hear, perhaps because it's funny and very few people do it. Inspired by that comment, the group of builders listed above from the Valorian Minecraft Server took on the task to make a Dirt house look good, and boy did they!

ITALIAN VILLA • BY RAPTORANKA: RaptorAnka is a builder of modern homes and buildings in Minecraft, and this particular gem comes from the famed World of Keralis server (www. keralis.net).

DREADFORT PALACE • PIRATE FORT BY JEFE070: The "residence of the Pirate Lord of the Iron Shore," this is a mighty, commanding wooden castle that sits alone atop the ocean, waiting for the ships of its pirate fleet to return with plunder and tales of conquest.

NORDIC FORT • BY WATCHMANT: This fort is meant to be a practical, utilitarian style with little in the way of a nod to artifice or decoration, but we still think it looks very nice.

WATER VILLAGE • BY KALYM: Sort of a fort/village, this build has a very unique feature in its very large open air entrance guarded by two hulking pirate ships. The entrance just barely breaks the water, so we guess it's a good thing that there aren't any hurricanes in Minecraft (yet!).

SKYTASTIC! • BY REVOLUSION_MINECRXFT: A colorful, fun-themed build, Skytastic! features multiple areas like you might find in a real theme park, including a kid's zone and, of course, a roller coaster or two.

DIRT HOUSE

OLANN ISLAND • BY ENMAH: The very popular Olann Island build has just about everything you could want in terms of entertainment, including planes, boats, coasters, and, as you see here, maybe the nicest looking casino we've come across.

SPHAGHETTI ROLLER COASTER BY DELICIOUSPANCAKE: Things you can expect in this western-themed roller coaster map: explosions, a four minute long ride, jugglin', lamps that fly about and a whole, whole lot more of sweet steampunk houses.

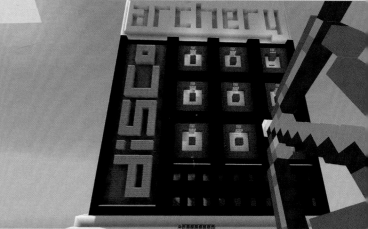

DISCO ARCHERY • BY FVDISCO: Along with SethBling, FVDisco is one of the most famous and prolific Redstone professionals in the world. Here we have FVDisco's very fun automatic archery range.

EDAWG878 • SERVER ADDRESS: EDAWG878.COM: A young creative server, edawg878 is great for those that want to join a plot-based (meaning you claim a plot of land on a grid as your own, as do others around your plot) server that has yet to get too extensive.

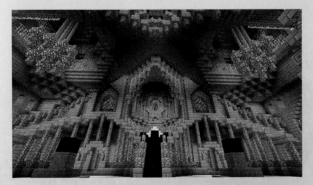

THE SHOTBOW NETWORK • SERVER ADDRESS: US.SHOTBOW.NET: Like Lichcraft and the Arkham Network, The Shotbow Network is one of the most extensive collections of minigame, PvP, and competition servers. For instance, here you see the Shotbow arcade, where you can find games like Light Bikes, a Tron-style fight to the death on a grid with motorcycles that leave a wall behind them.

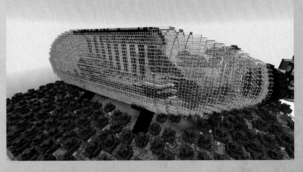

TREASURE ISLAND • SERVER ADDRESS: CREATIVEFREEBUILD.ORG: On Treasure Island's Creative Freebuild you'll find all of humanity's creativity on display and will run across everything from peaceful nature scenes, to bizarre creations like giant chairs, to this cool ship in a bottle.

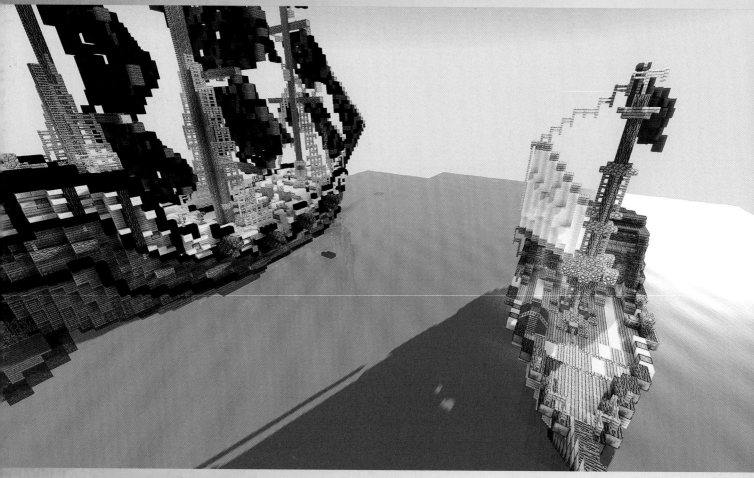

HYPIXEL (AND TEAM) • HYPIXEL.NET: Hypixel is a major force in the Minecraft community due to his immense skill-set when it comes to builds of all types, but most especially those that allow players to have a bit of competition with each other.

MURPS • PLANETMINECRAFT.COM/MEMBER/MURPS/: Utilizing nature, color, and organic-looking styles into their excellent fantastical builds, Murps creates environments that could not have come from any other builder.

THE HEXBOX • YOUTUBE.COM/USER/THEHEXBOX: TheHexBox's dedication to becoming a better and better modern home-builder is not only admirable, it's also led to the player becoming one of Minecraft's golden children of the modern house build.

BEACHSIDE HOTEL: Actually part of a much larger map, this hotel is so nicely crafted that it actually feels usable and alive.

ICE DRAGON: Dragons are everywhere in Minecraft, but few get the details like the tendons in the wings down as well as this one.

SOCCER STADIUM: Another popular style of build, stadiums can be very simple, or they can be full of realistic detail like this gorgeous example.

WAY TO THE FUTURE MAP • BY CHIA: Once again, a builder comes along and shows us that intense creativity doesn't always mean builds so big they bust graphics cards. In this case, it's builder Cihla with the Way to the Future map.

LE LABYRINTHE DE ZEPHIRR • BY MINECRAFTZEPHIRR: Mazes are something you see a lot of in Minecraft builds, as is Redstone, but a Redstone maze that builds itself as you go completely randomly? There aren't many of those, and Le Labyrinthe de Zephirr may be one of the most fascinating ones yet created.

PETER'S WORKING IPHONE • BY PETER–: You read that title right, and seeing this thing in action is even more impressive than it sounds. This gigantic iPhone really does have a touchscreen (made using some proximity sensor trickery), changes depending on what options you pick, and has 12 apps to run.

SERENITY • BY MRFRUITTREE: MrFruitTree is one of the world's premier modern house Minecraft builders. Check out the way the decorative beams on the second story window mirror the step-ladder-esque roof of the house.

STEAMPUNK CITY • BY GRAVI'TEAM: Set on the side of a cliff, this city has steam pouring out of it at every point. There are even paddle-boats that use steam!

BAUMHAUS • BY PORKCHOP MEDIA: At some point, just about everyone tries a treehouse or two, and it always seems like it will be an easy thing to do. Give it a shot though, and you know that pulling off a house that sits so nicely in a pre-existing tree like the Baumhaus does is rather tricky to pull off.

SAILOR'S HIDEOUT • BY SHADY OG OLA: Asymmetry is one of the hardest things to pull off in building, but it's also one of the most attractive when done right. This build seems to us to be right out of the 1800s, and we imagine pirates or other sailors stopping off for a rest here while on a long, long journey.

BABYLON • BY ROI_LOUIS: Taking his cue from ancient history and mythology, Roi_Louis created this quite huge city of Babylon. We love when people are inspired to this degree!

FUTURISTIC CITY • BY MCFRARCHITECT: Not one building from this city looks like anything out of our current world, yet somehow the team kept a continuous look throughout each that ties the whole thing together and makes it feel like it could exist.

CIVITATEM AQUA • BY JANIE177: Civitatem Aqua literally means Civilization (of) Water in Latin, and that is no mere brag when it comes to janie177's build. This thing is incredibly big, with a massive above-water structure leading to what feels like endless halls and underwater tunnels, each of which is decorated individually.

OCEAN FUTURE OF MANKIND • BY WATERIJSJE: Many builds are pretty long, but this one puts almost all others to shame at 1,000 blocks from end to end. It's meant to be a futuristic/sci-fi style water base, and it looks incredible from the inside, with an interesting mottled floor that seems to be meant as a sort of moisture farm or the like.

CUBE WORLD V2 • BY TYKEN132: When we saw the Cube World V2, we couldn't believe we'd never thought of recreating the natural world of Minecraft gone sideways. What's required in this build is pretty interesting: Tyken132 had to learn exactly how each natural feature is built by the game's algorithm, and then literally turn those ideas on their side.

▲ Little fun projects like this water elevator make your home more fun and easier to use, and they'll teach you good lessons on how to get things done in Minecraft.

COOL STARTER PROJECTS AND INVENTIONS

If you're looking for something fun to build in your Minecraft world, or something to make your life in the game a bit easier, well you came to the right chapter. This is a small selection of projects to try out that are fun to build and which will teach you a bit more about the game, while also being very useful. Plus, we'll give you some ideas for creating cool bases and buildings!

Inventions!

Each of these projects is something that does a specific task in your Minecraft world, from getting rid of pesky unwanted items, to helping you defeat Creepers and trick your friends.

The Infinite Water Well

No home is complete without one. The infinite water well is incredibly simple, but it's also one of the inventions that you're going to find yourself using time and time again. It puts a pool of water wherever you like it, and it will fill back up forever, no matter how many Buckets you take from it.

1. Pick up two Buckets worth of water, then go to where you want your infinite water well.

2. Dig a 2x2 square wherever you'd like your well.

3. Take one Bucket of Water and pour it out into one corner of the hole, then pour the other Bucket of Water into the corner that's diagonally opposite. The flowing water will soon go still, and you'll have water forever!

The Water Elevator

They're not exactly the most realistic architectural feature you're going to have in your house, but when you need to go up and down a long way quickly and without having to spend a lot of resources or time building a Ladder or Stairs, you will want a Water elevator.

1. These are super easy! First, find a place where you want to be able to go from high to low (or the other way around). Make sure that there is a ledge that goes straight down from where you are to where you want to get. If there isn't a straight down drop, dig so that there is one.

2. Drop a Bucket of Water so that it drops right down from your high spot to your low spot.

3. Go down to where the Water lands, and build a little square pool around the waterfall to catch the Water. We like to build ours right up on the Water, but you can make as big of a pool as you like.

4. Now you can jump into your Water elevator and either fall to the low spot, or hold the jump button to ride it to the top!

The Trashcan

Pesky, pesky Gravel and Dirt, always filling up our inventories! Well those days are gone with the newfangled home Trashcan. The Trashcan uses the properties of certain materials to permanently destroy items.

1. Get a bucket of Lava.

2. Find a place in your home (or outside it) where you want to throw things away and there's a wall (if outside, build a wall a couple blocks high).

3. Cut a block out where the wall meets the floor, then the block immediately below that one, and then two out from there.

4. Then build Cobblestone walls on the sides of the trench you made.

5. Point at the first space you cut into the wall (the one a single block above the ground), and dump the Lava so that it flows down into the trench.

6. Now you can just throw items into the Lava, and they'll be destroyed!

The Creeper Trap

Redstone is the system in Minecraft that's kind of like electricity, and it's one of the harder things to master in the game. However, there are some Redstone inventions you can make without having to learn all of the crazy, complicated Redstone rules. This is one of the most fun ones: an Arrow-launching Creeper attacking machine!

1. Build a Dispenser and a Lever, and craft a stack of Arrows. The Dispenser will take a Bow and one Redstone Dust.

2. Place the Dispenser where you'd like to shoot Creepers from. We think it's fun to put one in the wall next to our Door.

3. Fill the Dispenser with the Arrows.

4. Place the Lever on the back of the Dispenser.

5. Flip the Lever, and an Arrow will fire! It will keep firing as fast as you can flip, until you run all out of Arrows and have to go pick them up.

▲ **Simple TNT traps are fun and also quite funny, though only beginner players will be fooled by them.**

Miner's First TNT Trap

TNT traps are without question the most popular way for miners to get a trick attack on other miners, mostly because it's very funny to see a friend (or foe) surprised by an explosion! This is the Pressure Plate TNT trap, the most basic explosive trap in the game.

1. Start by digging a hole two blocks deep, then putting a TNT block at the bottom.

2. Put a block of another material on top of the TNT block, and then put a Pressure Plate on that. When players run over, a few seconds later the area will blow up.

Screenshot: Minecraft® ™ & © 2009–2016 Mojang/Notch.

Buildings!

Trying to think of something cool and big to build? Try one of these ideas out!

· Build a tower with a staircase that runs along the inside walls. Harder than you think! A hint: build the Stairs first, then the walls around them once you've reached as high as you want to go.

· Create a Great Pit to the Bedrock. A Great Pit is a big square hole that goes all the way down to the Bedrock level and has a Ladder, a Water Elevator, or stairs to get up and down it. Not only do these look pretty neat, they're also really helpful when mining, because you have easy access to every level of rock in the game. Remember to never dig straight down, though, or you may accidently fall in lava!

▲ At some point in your Pit, build a little base so that you don't have to go all the way up to your main base constantly.

▲ A completed Water base from the outside.

· Try and create an underwater base. It's tricky, but you can build a base that is totally under the ocean. The hard part is being able to breathe and see down there, but you can use a few tricks to do this. Bring some Glowstone with you for light, and also bring some Fences and Doors. Both of these items create a pocket of air around them when placed, so you can put some down where you're building and swim back to them to get some air.

THE GREAT MINECRAFT CHALLENGE

▲ Skeletons are easy to defeat compared to some of the mobs you'll have to fight to complete this challenge list.

Think you're pretty good at Minecraft? This is the official Minecraft for Kids Challenge List— a series of difficult challenges in the game that will give even the most expert crafters a run for their money.

See how many you can complete, and wow your friends with your incredible Minecrfatin' skills, you cool crafter.

Try to accomplish each of these goals, and keep track of your overall score.

5 Points (Easy)

- Download a map online and explore it
- Win a round of Spleef!
- Find your first Structure
- Tame a Horse
- Play with three or more friends at once

10 Points (Medium)

- Build a Nether home
- Build a moat all the way around your house out of Water or Lava
- Build a tower from the Bedrock to the sky limit
- Visit all dimensions

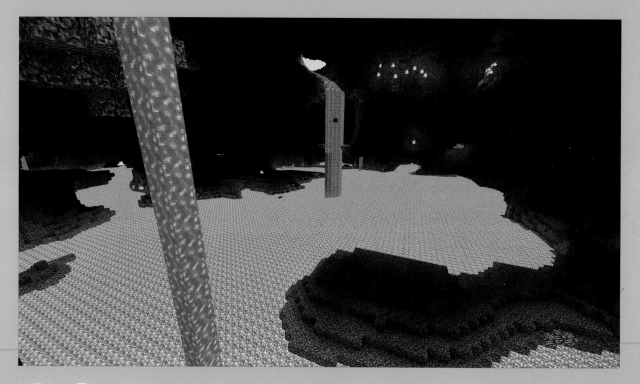

20 Points (Hard)

- **Create a solid Block of each type of ore (Expert Bonus for 50 points: create a house out of Blocks of Diamond!)**

- **Get a Skeleton to kill a Creeper**

- **Screenshot the hardest to find mobs in Minecraft: a Spider Jockey, a Charged Creeper, and a Wither**

- **"Beat" the game by visiting The End and defeating the Ender Dragon**

- **Defeat one of every kind of mob, including the Wither and the Ender Dragon**

- **Defeat enough Creepers to make a full stack of TNT**

- **Craft a full set of Diamond Armor and a Diamond Sword**

- **Find and clear out an Abandoned Mineshaft**

MASTER BUILDER
JUNIOR